Developed and produced by Ripley Publishing Ltd

This edition published and distributed by:
Mason Crest Publishers Inc.
370 Reed Road, Broomall, Pennsylvania 19008
(866) MCP-BOOK (toll free)
www.masoncrest.com

Ripley's Believe It or Not!
Was That a Good Idea
ISBN 978-1-4222-1543-2
Library of Congress Cataloging-in-Publication data is available

Ripley's Believe It or Not!—Complete 16 Title Series
ISBN 978-1-4222-1529-6

PUBLISHER'S NOTE
While every effort has been made to verify the accuracy of the entries in this book,
the Publishers cannot be held responsible for any errors contained in the work.
They would be glad to receive any information from readers.

WARNING
Some of the stunts and activities in this book are undertaken by experts and should not
be attempted by anyone without adequate training and supervision.

Printed in the United States of America

Ripley's Believe It or Not!

WAS THAT A GOOD IDEA

PUBLISHING

a Jim Pattison Company

Was That A Good Idea?

You'll be surprised! The wacky feats and

peculiar inventions in this book will leave you

wanting more. Meet the extreme artist who

defies death by performing handstands in crazy

places, the dog that regularly hang-glides,

and the contortionist who can dislocate his

entire body to fit through a tennis racket.

Buddy the Labrador enjoys
hang-gliding with his
owner...

Inflated nNovaTion!

NOW HERE'S AN invention you can drink to—the first inflatable pub!

The traveling tavern can hold up to 30 visitors at a time. English designer Andi Francis worked on the idea for nine months after deciding to create a drinks marquee with a bit more flare than a beer tent.

The interior of the blow-up bar has everything you might expect in the real thing. It comes complete with fireplace (which is, of course, purely decorative), a stuffed fish mounted on one wall, mock Tudor beams, and lattice windows.

The Pub

Hot-desking

OIAB (Office in a Bucket) is the ideal solution for any company boss wanting to give his staff a change of scenery. Simply pick your spot—maybe the park or even the beach—and the office can be inflated in just eight minutes.

Blue Sky Thinking

The inflatable office can be inflated wherever you like—in parks, gardens, or even on a rooftop—to provide workers with a change of scenery and fresh inspiration every day.

Out of Sight
Henry Bayerl of Portsmouth, Ohio, managed to completely overhaul a car while wearing a blindfold.

Breach of the Peace
A concert composed by Luciano Berio was once held to promote world peace. Unfortunately halfway through the concert, a cannon was fired that injured several people in the audience and then caused a riot to break out.

Big Shot
One time when General George Custer was hunting buffalo, he accidentally shot his own horse!

Cutting Corners
Sami Sure, a construction worker in Beirut, Lebanon, couldn't afford to pay his barber 65 cents for a shave, so he gave him half of his lottery ticket instead. The ticket won and the barber scooped $133,000.

From a Scream to a Whisper
Ever wanted to scream out loud during a stressful situation? Well now you can with an invention that allows the "stressee" to shout into a small ball that is filled with special foam. The foam muffles the noise, making it seem like a whisper.

Bullet-proof Pizza
When Cole Woolner of Michigan was delivering two deep-dish pizzas, his life was saved—by the pizzas! A bullet hit the pies and missed him.

Pup, Pup, and Away
Buddy the Labrador and his owner, Bill Kimball of San Diego, California, have been hang-gliding together for more than eight years. Buddy's first flight took place when he was a six-month-old pup. Since then, he has joined Bill on more than 75 flights.

Give and Take

In 1795, Boston millionaire James Swan paid off the American national debt to France, a total of $2,024,900, from his own pocket! However, he spent the last 22 years of his life in jail, as the French government sent him to Saint Pelagie Prison for debtors.

Mississippi Blues

Instead of taking his vehicle to a proper car wash, a man from Hannibal, Missouri, decided to save money by cleaning it in the nearby Mississippi River. He carefully backed it into a foot of water, but when he got out to start washing it, the car floated away. The police later recovered it some way downstream.

Blowing Hot and Cold

A British man got more than he bargained for when his lips became stuck to the lock on his car door while he was blowing on it in order to defrost it!

Gone Fishing

The "Aquariass," which attaches to a working toilet, is a quirky cistern fitted with a real aquarium. But don't worry, the fish aren't actually flushed away!

Name Dropping

Cleston Jenkins of Kentucky had the first names of each of his seven ex-wives tattooed on his arm.

Money Matters

In April 2000, the Brazilian government issued bank-notes made of plastic!

Eyes Like a Hawk

An excited birdwatcher used CB radio to bring birders flocking to a field on the Isles of Scilly, off the southwest of England, to see a nighthawk, a rare visitor from America. Only when telescopes and binoculars were trained on it did it become apparent that the "rare bird" was in fact a cowpat!

Musical Chairs

Some people sing in the shower, some even sing on the toilet, but fancy having a toilet sing to you! This singing loo, by Swiss inventors Reto Marogg and Roger Weisskopf, was presented at the annual exhibition of inventions in Geneva.

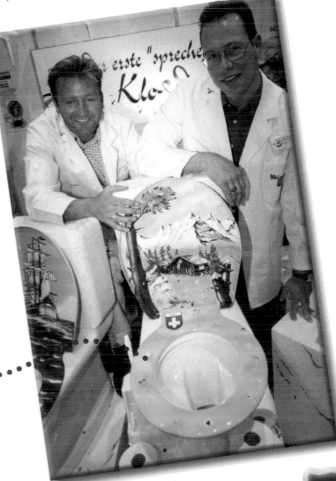

Talk is Cheap

Unable to find a summer job, teenager Trevor Dame tried to earn money by giving out advice on a street corner in his hometown of Kelowna, British Columbia. Aware that his advice might not be of the highest quality, he wore a sign around his neck saying, "Mediocre advice— 25 cents."

Wake-up Call

In 1907, a patent was filed for an alarm clock that sprays water onto the face of a sleeping person.

Get Back to Your Roots

Scientists developed these multi-colored carrots to encourage more people to eat their vegetables. Not only that, but the modified carrots are actually better for you, due to the healthy pigments used to change their color.

Clean and Sober

After stealing cash from a Colorado Springs corner store, an armed robber demanded a bottle of whiskey from the shelf. The clerk refused to serve him because he didn't believe he was 21. To prove he was, the robber obligingly showed the clerk his driver's licence—bearing his full name and address.

U.S.A. Oklahoma

It is illegal for women to do their own hair without being licensed by the state.

Snake Bite
Jack Bibby actually put live rattlesnakes in his mouth.

Cuddling Up

IF YOU'RE USED to a cuddle at bedtime, these pillows might help for nights when you're alone.

Made in Japan, the Lap Pillow and My Boyfriend's Arm Pillow are designed for those who are most comfortable sleeping next to someone else. They help you to sleep by simulating the shape of an absent loved-one.

The Lap Pillow is shaped like a kneeling woman and comes with either a red or black skirt.

11

Playing with Fire

Bestselling children's novelist, G.P. Taylor accidentally burned three of his manuscripts. While clearing out his house in preparation for moving, Taylor mistook the original manuscripts for old paperwork and burned them to cinders. One of them, which had gone on to sell in excess of 250,000 copies, was given a $150,000 (£100,000) value by a collector prior to the incident.

The manuscripts Taylor accidentally burned were for three of his bestselling novels: Shadowmancer, Wormwood, *and* Tersias.

The Finger of Suspicion

When arrested in 2003, a Nigerian man chewed off his own fingertips so his prints couldn't be taken. He soaked his fingers in the jail toilet, then chewed away the softened skin.

Early Warning System

A man went into a McDonald's in Sydney, Australia, at 8:50 a.m. one day in 2000, produced a gun, and demanded cash. The girl serving said she couldn't open the till without a food order. So the robber ordered a Big Mac, but was told that they weren't available until 10:30 because only the breakfast menu was being offered at that time. Frustrated, the gunman gave up and walked out.

An Unscheduled Flight

An airport baggage-handler made an unscheduled flight from Dallas to Mexico in 2001 after accidentally locking himself in the plane's cargo hold. Crew members reported hearing a knocking sound at Dallas, but weren't able to trace it.

Pulling a Fast One

A 41-year-old man from Barrie, Canada, who pretended to be a traffic policeman was sentenced to six months in jail after pulling over a real detective for speeding.

Pot Shot

J.G. Levack, an exhibition shooter from Connecticut, tossed a golf ball in the air and hit it with a rifle bullet. He did this with such accuracy that it landed on a green with 150 yd (137 m) distance.

Finger Stuck

An Illinois man who got his finger stuck in a payphone for three hours was taken to the hospital with the phone still attached to his hand. Passers-by, fire crews, and a workman from the phone company all failed to free him, until eventually, paramedics cut the phone from its base and took the man—and the phone—to the hospital.

Natural Wastage

Government officials in Sydney, Nova Scotia, spent $410,000 erecting a fence topped with barbed wire around a toxic-waste site in 2001. Since they fixed it so that the barbed wire faced inward, the fence allowed easy access to the hazardous site but then trapped trespassers inside!

By Hook or by Crook

A 36-year-old man who robbed an Ontario discount store was quickly arrested, mainly because he made no attempt to disguise the metal hook that he used in place of a hand.

A Lingering Kiss

A pair of teenagers kissing in their car at traffic lights in Rio de Janeiro, Brazil, held up traffic for two-and-a-half hours when their dental braces became entwined.

By the Skin of his Teeth
Sri Lankan farmer Gamini Wasantha Kumara displays extraordinary pulling power. Gamini is seen here biting down on a harness in preparation for his train-pulling challenge at Colombo's main railway station in 2001.

In Training
Gamini Wasantha Kumara pulled the 40-ton railway carriage a total of more than 80 ft (25 m) in Colombo, Sri Lanka, using only the harness gripped between his teeth!

Duty Calls

Passengers on a flight from Zurich, Switzerland, to London panicked when it was announced that the plane was about to crash in the ocean. Then the captain explained that they had played the wrong tape: "We meant to tell you we were about to serve the duty-free products," he said.

Opening Shelved

In Gloucestershire, England, a council had to inform residents that a new $3-million (£2-million) library would not be opening on schedule in 2003 because the council had forgotten to order any books or shelves!

Sleeping Partner

In 2002, a Romanian retiree ran up a bill of $1,800—the equivalent of the average annual salary in Romania—after falling asleep while on a phone chat line.

Under the Knife

A man from Chino Valley, Arizona, who had been playing with a knife by tossing it into the air, was taken to the hospital with a 12-in (30-cm) steak knife firmly embedded in the back of his head.

The Milk of Human Kindness

A woman in Nanjin, China, ordered 3,000 barrels of milk over a three-month period in the name of a local university as she feared that her boyfriend, a dairy company sales manager, would be recalled to their head office due to poor milk sales.

Balancing Act
A.C. Johnson of Kansas balanced an egg on a piece of chicken wire.

Log Jam

Kenneth Lambert of New Hampshire crossed the log-jammed Androscoggin River on snow skis.

Taking the Plunge

DIVING 29 FT (9 m) into water may not sound too challenging, but it certainly is when the water is only 12 in (30 cm) deep!

Louisiana-born diver Danny Higginbottom took the plunge in front of spectators in London, England, and earned himself a place in the record books for his splashing feat!

Injury Time

There were so many injuries during 2004's Women's National Festival of Rugby in Staffordshire, England, that emergency services termed it "a major incident." Ten ambulances and a helicopter dealt with ruptured muscles, broken bones, and even a dislocated hip.

Double Bass
Arthur K. Ferris of Ironia, New Jersey, built a 14-ft (4.25-m) high bass fiddle.

Blast Off
Wanting a gas stove for her apartment, a San Francisco woman stole one from a neighboring building—without first turning off the gas. She caused a $200,000 explosion.

Break a Leg
Charles Grubbs and Melody Wyman had set their hearts on being married at the top of Mount Rainier, Washington State, but on their way up the mountain for the 2002 ceremony, high winds blew them and their minister into a crevasse. After a visit to hospital, the wedding went ahead as planned—except that the bride had a plaster cast on her leg and needed the aid of a crutch.

Blank Looks
A counterfeiter in Paramount, California, did a sterling job preparing money that he tried to pass on to a store owner. There was just one giveaway: the back of the bills was completely blank.

What a Giveaway
Los Angeles police got lucky with a robbery suspect who just couldn't keep his mouth shut. When detectives asked each man in the line-up to repeat the words, "Give me all your money or I'll shoot," the guilty man shouted: "That's not what I said!"

Hide and Seek
A British woman sparked a full-scale police search, complete with helicopter, for her three-year-old daughter in 2004—when the child was behind a couch the whole time. It was estimated that the search cost $45,000 (£30,000).

U.S.A.
Ohio

Any map that does not have Lima clearly stated on it cannot be sold.

Breaking the Ice
Sri Lankan farmer Gamini Wasantha Kumara endured having no fewer than 50 blocks of ice dropped on him from a height of 17 ft (5 m). Gamini laid with a block of granite weighing 440 lb (200 kg) on his chest, while the blocks of ice, each weighing a further 110 lb (50 kg), were dropped on top of him, one at a time.

Gamini Wasantha Kumara has made several attempts to get into Ripley's record books with his various feats.

Between a Rock and a Hard Place
No stranger to heights or handstands, Eskil Ronningsbakken balances on four stacked chairs at more than 3,000 ft (1,000 m) above sea level in Norway.

Hit the Roof
Extreme artist Eskil Ronningsbakken does a handstand on top of the 280-ft (86-m) high Radisson S.A.S. Scandinavia Building in Copenhagen, Denmark.

A Real Cliff-hanger
Eskil Ronningsbakken performing his trademark handstand without a safety net 2,000 ft (600 m) above sea level at Pulpit Cliff, Norway.

It's in the Bag

Hoping to look inconspicuous, a bank robber in Portland, Oregon, handed the teller a note ordering her to put all the money in a paper bag. She read the note, wrote on the bottom, "I don't have a paper bag," and handed it back to the raider. His plan foiled, he fled empty-handed.

Topple That!

Captain W. E. Wyatt from Fort Worth, Texas, used 84 dominoes for this feat in 1931. The steady-handed police officer managed to stack 83 dominoes on top of the single vertical one!

When You're in a Hole...

After six months of digging a secret tunnel from Saltillo Prison, Mexico, 75 convicts made their daring bid for freedom, only to find that their tunnel emerged in the nearby courtroom where many of them had been sentenced. The surprised judges quickly sent them back to jail.

Mummy's Boy

A 22-year-old Los Angeles man advertised in a magazine as a lonely Romeo looking for a girl to accompany him on vacation to South America. Alas, the first reply he received turned out to be from his widowed mother!

Badge of Dishonor

A would-be robber of a Texas grocery store disguised his face with a ski mask, but forgot to remove from his breast pocket a laminated badge that bore his name, place of employment, and position within the company—an oversight spotted by witnesses.

Lost in Translation

An elderly American tourist had to be rescued from woodland in Bavaria, Germany, in 2004 after he got lost while using a 90-year-old guidebook.

Get your Facts Straight

A woman from Connecticut was identified in 2003 as the person who had robbed six banks after she called her local newspaper to complain about inaccuracies in their reports of her robberies.

What's the Hold-up?

A man robbed a bank in Briarwood, West Virginia, in 2004 by taping a "stick-up" note to the teller's window. He was arrested when he later returned to the same window because he had forgotten to pick up the note!

Seed Drill

Taiwanese artist Chen Forng-Shean wrote this 28-character poem by ancient Chinese poet Su Tung-po on a sesame seed! When the seed is placed on the face of George Washington on a $1 bill, the scale of the writing can be fully appreciated.

No Strings Attached

Contortionist Captain Frodo, a member of the Circus Oz, dislocates certain bones in his body to enable him to pass his body through a tennis racket as part of his performance!

Turn Yourself In

After robbing an Ohio convenience store in 2004, a man hijacked a car and led police on a high-speed chase before taking a wrong turn and driving into a police station parking lot.

A Night to Remember

Residents of the Romanian village of Cristinesti fled their homes in panic in 2004 after mistaking disco lights in a nearby town for an alien invasion!

Finger of Fate

A man in Modesto, California, was arrested for trying to hold up a Bank of America branch without a weapon. He used a thumb and finger to simulate a gun, but forgot to keep his hand in his pocket.

Airline Food

A group of vintage aviation enthusiasts left their plane in a field near Hereford, England, while they went to lunch in a nearby pub. When they returned, they found the 1948 Auster airplane being eaten by cows! The animals caused thousands of dollars of damage by chewing a large hole in the fuselage.

BenT Out of ShApE

DONALD HAMBLY can bend iron bars using only his neck!

Putting great faith in the Shaolin monk meditation he practices, Donald positions the bars against his throat and gradually moves forward, bending them as he goes.

The steel rods could puncture Donald's throat at any time during the act, but his skill and concentration ensure his safety.

To begin with, the bars are moved into place and Donald starts to push!

He stays tense and alert as the bars gradually bend in the middle.

It starts to give as he applies pressure against the bars.

One final push toward the end, and he's almost there!

Stone the Crows!
Mistaking it for a Viking settlement, archeologists excavated an ordinary 1940s patio in a back garden in Fife, Scotland.

Other Fish to Fry
Firefighters in Baton Rouge, Louisiana, burned down their own fire station after leaving fish frying on a stove when they were called out to attend a blaze.

A Hiding to Nothing
A Romanian man sentenced for fraud in 1994 hid in his parents' basement for eight years—to avoid a three-and-a-half-year jail sentence.

Unlucky Number
Sentenced to seven years in jail, a man from San Antonio, Texas, begged the judge not to give him seven years because seven was his unlucky number. So the judge gave him eight years.

Caught Out
Two burglars fled from a building in Florida in 2003 and jumped into what they thought was their getaway car, only to find that it was an unmarked police car!

Barbie World
As part of a promotion for Barbie, all the houses in this street in Manchester, England, were temporarily painted bright pink!

A Nasty Shock
A man in Kitwe, Zambia, was electrocuted in 2000 when, having run out of space on his clothes line, he unwisely decided to hang the remainder of his wet washing on a live power line that passed his house.

Double Trouble
A year after crashing into Jim Hughes' yacht near Portsmouth, England, and causing $30,000 (£20,000) damage, Icelandic sailor Eriker Olafsson still felt guilty. So he decided to return to the harbor and make a full apology, only to hit Mr. Hughes' yacht again and postpone his plans for a round-the-world voyage for a second time!

A Cut Above
Joe Horowitz from Los Angeles was able to balance an 18-lb (8-kg) saber on the end of his nose!

Triumphant Stag
An American poacher who shot a stag standing above him on an overhanging rock was killed instantly when the dead animal fell on him.

Wind Break
Frank Morosky of Cedar Rapids, Iowa, has made charcoal-lined diapers costing between $20 and $50, to reduce the odor of dogs' flatulence.

Puss in... Slippers
Japanese inventor Kenji Kawakami has conceived a pair of duster slippers to be worn by a cat, so that the animal can polish the floor while it walks!

On the Record
A pair of agitated robbers burst into a record store in Michigan, nervously waving guns. One shouted: "Nobody move!" When his accomplice moved, the first bandit shot him.

Denmark
Attempting to escape from prison is not actually illegal, although if recaptured, one is required to serve out the remainder of one's term.

Bare-faced Cheek
A Canadian man who was refused a ticket from Los Angeles to Australia in 2004, took off all his clothes, ran naked across the runway, and climbed into a plane's wheel well. Firefighters finally talked him out.

The Party's Over
After a party in 2001, a woman fell asleep on a mattress in an Alabama garbage bin—and woke hours later in a Georgia landfill 20 mi (30 km) away. She narrowly escaped being crushed by a garbage compactor.

Heavy Duty
Weighing 147 lb (67 kg), Stephen Stoyan made two successive push-ups with 285 lb (129 kg) on his back.

Courtroom Drama
A computer error resulted in an eight-year-old boy from New Jersey being summoned for jury service in 2001. It was the second time Kyle Connor had been called up to serve on a jury, the first being when he was five. Kyle said he was perfectly happy to try it, as long as the judge didn't mind!

Tooth and Nail
A dentist soon got to the root of Patrick Lawler's toothache—a 4-in (10-cm) nail that the construction worker had embedded in his skull six days earlier! A nail gun had backfired while he was working at a Colorado ski resort, sending one nail into a piece of wood, and another through his mouth and 1½ in (4 cm) into his brain.

Pressing the Limits

REV. JON BRUNEY from Fremont, Indiana, performs radical exhibitions of strength as part of his "Pressing the Limits" event.

His strongman activities include breaking flaming bricks, crushing a full can of soda, and inflating a hot-water bottle until it explodes. In July 2004, Jon was one of three strongmen to pull a 15-ton semi-tractor trailer for a distance of 1 mi (1.5 km)! The trailer was loaded with the band Bledsoe, who performed on the flatbed of the truck.

Jon lays under a bed of 3,000 nails, as a woman jumps rope on top of the wooden board. Afterward, the audience could see nail indentations in Jon's skin, but no sign of more serious physical injury.

Jon Bruney bends a steel bar against the top of his head, during one of his motivational performances.

To illustrate his sheer strength, Jon is able to tear entire phone books in half!

"Little Giant" Eddie Polo.
Pulling a car by his hair 100 yds
1 minute 40 seconds Dover N.H. Aug 23/1937

Tearing his Hair Out
"Little Giant" Eddie Polo pulls a car 100 yd (90 m) in 1 minute 40 seconds in Dover, New Hampshire, in August 1937—using only the strength of his hair.

Economy Drive
Resenting the prospect of paying a $55 delivery fee on his new lawnmower, a man from Plainville, Connecticut, decided instead to drive it home along the road at a top speed of 12 mph (20 km/h). Far from saving money, he was fined $78 for driving an unregistered vehicle!

A Lost Cause
A tourist from Toledo, Washington, on holiday in Germany in 2003, relied solely on his car's automatic navigation system to steer him around the unfamiliar roads of Bavaria… until it led him straight through the doors of a supermarket. The tourist, who said he didn't even see the supermarket doors, came to a halt when he crashed into shelves.

Life's a Beach
One bank of the River Seine is turned into a beach each summer so that Parisians can enjoy the sunshine without having to trek to the coast. The mayor had the "Paris Plage" developed to include palm trees, sand, and a swimming pool.

Growing Room
A German firm has developed a shoe that grows to keep pace with children's feet. At the press of a button, the shoe increases by one size by expanding like an accordion.

On the Fiddle
Ontario police charged a motorist with careless driving after catching him playing the violin while at the wheel. The 54-year-old man said he was warming up for a concert.

Having a Ball
The Stade de France stadium in Paris was transformed into a beach in July 2002 with 100,000 sq ft (9,000 sq m) of sand. Visitors could play ball games or simply relax in deckchairs.

Bear the Blow

IF BASEBALL BATS and cars are no match for this super suit, then a grizzly bear doesn't stand much chance of getting through either!

Troy Hurtubise of North Bay, Canada, tested the strength of his specially made protective suit at the Ripley's museum in St. Augustine, Florida.

The suit is designed to help nature photographers get closer than ever before to bears in the wild, without the fear of being mauled by them.

The tests Troy's suit endured included being hit repeatedly with steel baseball bats by members of the audience, and even being hit by a swinging car! Troy is seen here sitting among a pile of bricks that were previously a wall. The car was swung at him and hit him in the chest. He was knocked down but otherwise unhurt, while the wall was smashed.

Coffee Break

Civet coffee was developed as a luxurious option for the adventurous. The coffee is processed in the digestive tract from the civet cat of Sumatra. The cat eats the coffee beans, which are then hand-picked from its droppings. The coffee costs the princely sum of $21 (£14) for an ounce because only 1,100 lb (500 kg) of it are made every year. However, experts genuinely enjoy the taste. One Dutch connoisseur described it as having a fine chocolate aroma that gives a delicious taste at the back of the throat.

Even if you're a coffee-lover, you might have the same reaction as this when you discover how civet coffee is made!

The Name of the Game

When Californian artist Maria Alquilar painted a $40,000 mural outside a public library, little did she realize that it contained 11 misspelled names of historical giants including Einstein, Shakespeare, Van Gogh, and Michelangelo. It is thought to have cost around $6,000 to correct the mistakes.

O Brother!

Acting as his own lawyer in a Texas federal court, Adam Martin called his brother to the witness stand to testify to his good character. When Adam asked his brother if he had ever committed any crimes, his brother responded without hesitation: "Yeah. You were with me on four different bank robberies, Adam. You know that."

A Change of Key

Frankie Masters had a 12-member band, with a difference—each member played music on a manual typewriter. The overall effect sounded like a xylophone.

Banana Split

A Cincinnati-based firm is planning to market strawberry-flavored bananas! Chiquita International claims bananas taste boring.

Heaven Scent

These rose-scented stamps were used on letters in Thailand in 2002. Printed in England, they were released in Bangkok in February to commemorate St. Valentine's Day.

Dozy Burglar

It was bad enough that a burglar chose to break into the offices of the police department in Oxnard, California, but to make matters worse, he then fell asleep! Bemused police discovered him when they arrived for work in the morning, and promptly made him the first arrest of the day.

I Want to Ride My Tricycle

Bobby Jordan and six of his friends, who call themselves the "Descanso Big Wheel Boys," consider themselves Big Wheel daredevils—despite being adults. For the last year, the full-grown men have been getting their thrills by racing their toy tricycles down steep California mountainsides. They typically reach 35 mph (55 km/h), which causes the plastic wheels to disintegrate long before they reach the bottom.

Going to the Dogs

Tina and Kate, two dogs living in Somerset, England, inherited £450,000 ($670,000) when their owner passed away. The inheritance was enough for them to be able to enjoy a home and 4 acres (1.6 ha) of land in the village of Peasedown St. John.

Brace Yourself

Truck driver Herbert Scott from Burnley, England, in 1986 sought medical attention following a fall at work. As a result of a misunderstanding, he kept a neck brace on for the next 14 years instead of the four weeks that the doctors had advised.

Bird-brained

Thieves who stole 15 homing pigeons from bird-fancier Peter Ball of Berkshire, England, tried them out… and watched in despair as they flew straight back to Ball's loft!

The Color of Money

An unemployed American printer who turned to counterfeiting was caught because he used black ink instead of bright green on his phoney bills. It turned out that he was color-blind.

Fire Drill

When fire broke out at a restaurant in the Austrian city of Vienna in November 2003, the owner and staff quickly fled the building. In their haste, they forgot to evacuate the guests. Even though the dining room had filled with smoke, 20 people were still sitting at their tables when fire crews arrived.

It's a Dog's Life

These lucky pups are now looked after by gardener Henry Escott, who ensures that they have everything they need.

Giving Up the Ghost

In 2004, the ghost of Indiana man Collin Proctor, in the form of his walking-cane, was sold on auction website eBay for $65,100. Mary Anderson of Hobart, Indiana, put her father's ghost up for sale to help her young son to cope with his grandfather's death. She asked the buyer to write to the boy acknowledging receipt of the ghost. Sadly, the sale came back to haunt her as the resultant publicity gave her insomnia.

Tunnel Vision

The driver of this car was caught in a sticky situation after mistaking the entrance to the subway for a ramp into a parking garage in Paris, France. Firemen were called in to rescue the car from slipping further down into the underground tunnels.

The Price You Pay

A St. Louis janitor got his finger stuck in a payphone change slot and spent three hours trying to dislodge it while passers-by laughed at his predicament. He finally thought to use his free hand to call 911.

Sweet Dreams

A Japanese toy firm claims to have devised a gadget that can help people to control their dreams. They say the Dream Workshop can be programmed before bedtime to help sleepers choose who or what they want to dream about.

Chin Up

Robert Dotzauer from Los Angeles could balance three lawnmowers on his chin at the same time.

FeNdiNG Off ShArks

THANKS TO THE Shark Shield, shark attacks could soon become a thing of the past.

The new invention, from Australian company SeaChange Technology, emits an electronic field to repel sharks without harming them. It can be fitted to surfboards or to divers' legs to allow people to enjoy the water without risk of attack.

The device emits an electronic field that will cause nearby sharks to have muscular spasms. This will put them off venturing closer, but doesn't cause any lasting damage.

Emergency Service

Policemen who arrested a burglar on the roof of a bank in Kent, England, had to be rescued by fire crews after they became stuck.

In the Hot Seat

Around the time of the invention of the electric chair, an unwitting citizen in New York State offered to test the electric current in the chair: The current worked and the man's family received $5,000.

I'm All Ears

An exhibition, entitled "Show and Tel: the Art of Connection," held at the Zimmer Children's Museum in Los Angeles, California, included quirky designs such as this two-part ear-and-mouthpiece telephone by Robert Graham.

Zimmer Frame

"Commander Ian Zimmer," designed by Alan and Deborah Ladwig, is just one of the bizarre telephonic inventions that were on display.

Does It Bite?

Should you stroke it or answer it? The phones, like this one by Mauro Caputo, were later auctioned.

Ring My Bell

Wedding bells won't be the only bells ringing on this telephone, created by Jessica Trovato. The designers of the unusual creations at the exhibition included athletes, politicians, and celebrities, such as Elizabeth Taylor, Alicia Keys, and Paula Abdul.

Water World

If you're the type of person who envies the life of a fish, then the hemosponge invention may be just for you! It's an experimental device created by the U.S. Office of Naval Research, that extracts oxygen from the water, making it possible for divers to remain submerged for several days at a time.

Fall Guy

Brazilian Marcello Bonga made the first ever crossing by rope of the Iguazu waterfalls from the Brazilian side to the Argentinian side. He crossed the Devil's Throat section, using only a rope and a harness, as thousands of tons of water crashed beneath him.

InDex

ACKNOWLEDGMENTS

Jacket (t/r) Peter Brooker/Rex Features

4 Sam Barcroft/Rex Features; 6 (dp) Lewis Whyld/Rex Features; 7 (t/l) Lewis Whyld/Rex Features, (t/r, b/r) Inflate/Rex Features;
8 (b) Sam Barcroft/Rex Features; 9 (t/l) Rex Features, (b/r) Reuters; 10 (t/r) SON/NAP/Rex Features; 11 (sp) Kim Kyung-Hoon/Reuters,
(b/l) Yuriko Nakao/Reuters; 12 (t/r) United National Photographers/Rex Features; 13 (t/r, b) Anuruddha Lokuhapuarachchi/Reuters;
15 Nils Jorgensen/Rex Features; 16 (t/r) Anuruddha Lokuhapuarachchi/Reuters; 17 (sp) Allover Norway/Rex Features, (t/r) Soren
Nielsen/Rex Features, (b/r) Morten Nordby/Rex Features; 18 (b/l) Simon Kwong/Reuters; 19 (t/r, b/l) David Gray/Reuters; 22 (t/l)
Darren Banks/Rex Features, (c/r) Mike Poloway/Rex Features, (b) United National Photographers/Rex Features; 26 (b/l) Sipa Press/Rex
Features, (b/r) HOM/Rex Features; 28 (t) John Downing/Rex Features, (b/r) Sukree Sukplang/Reuters; 29 South West News Service/Rex
Features; 30 (t/l) Sipa Press/Rex Features; 31 Rex Features; 32 Peter Brooker/Rex Features; 33 Jon Super/Rex Features.

All other photos are from Ripley's Entertainment Inc.
Every attempt has been made to acknowledge correctly and contact copyright holders and we apologize
in advance for any unintentional errors or omissions, which will be corrected in future editions.